CHAPTER 1: THE CURSING	2
CHAPTER 2: DOING GOD THINGS	6
CHAPTER 3: THE GOOD OF THE WORLD	10
CHAPTER 4: THE GAMING PHASE	14
CHAPTER 5: THE RETURN OF THE ORIGINAL OBAMA	21
THE END!!!	24

INTRODUCTION

Bobar everyone! Welcome to bark No.2... I mean book No.2. But this tail oops I did it again (as Britney would say). But this tale made this world crumble like a cookie. This book is the one and only, Obama the Goofball. Oops! I'm making so many mistakes in this book. I mean Obama the God. It won't happen again. Now, similarly to the first book, Obama will be acting made. It's just that he has supe powers and you will find out how gets them later on in the book (a very happy book).

CHAPTER 1: THE CURSING

Obama was in his snuggly-monster-from-Jupiter blanket. He was sitting right there on Barney's sofa. You might remember Barney from the last book. All of a sudden, Obama wasn't there. He was opening the grand, the one and only...cheese box. He selects a cheesecake. Game on as the cheesecake battles for victory against Obama's mouth. Sadly, for the cheesecake, Obama's mouth won. It was a soft, fluffy, full-fat, vanilla cheesecake which Obama loved. It was so delicious that he decided to make the recipe public which you will find in another chapter.

Obama zoomed back to Barney, and he

was going to go out for his daily dog/monster/fly walk and see the people that still respected him for being a monster. The second he stepped out of the door; Obama was struck by yellow lightning. It hit him straight in the kneecap, which was weird, because monsters from Jupiter don't have kneecaps. It just hit him where his kneecap should've been which was very strange. He woke up in a dark hospital, but light at the same time, because Obama was not actually conscious. He was dreaming about the hospital where he actually was...spooky. In his dream, the nurse was a big, glowing light. The 'glowing light' nurse said to Obama, in a wispy tone, 'You are the one I have chosen. You are the one to hold the power. I give you, my power. Goodbye.'

Obama woke up (imagine someone clicking their fingers to represent the suddenness of him waking up). But the strange part was that he felt as if the lightning strike didn't happen. There was no intense pain in his 'not there' kneecap. He left with his things and went back to the Black House (for any of you who do not know, or haven't read the previous book, the Black House is Htrae's equivalent to Earth's White House (Htrae is the planet that Obama lives on)). Obama settled down and was just gazing at the TV channels...bored...with nothing to do, thinking about his insane dream. He wondered about what the glowing man said to him. He really wanted to know the answer, but Obama got distracted by his philosophy on thinking and now he wanted a drink of camembert. Yes, you read that right. A DRINK of camembert!!! He finished his cheese beverage, noisily slurping the last bit of grated cheese from the bottom of the grater he was drinking from.

Suddenly, very randomly, Mr. Man jumped from the ceiling, grabbed Obama and stuffed him into a giant pillowcase, made of pillowcases which were made of pillowcases – you get the idea. Mr. Man said, 'You have some grand powers. Do not give anyone emotional damage. You have powers known to man as *the god's death!*'.

Obama replies, 'How rude! I obviously have magical powers. I'm the president!'

Mr. Man said, 'No, not powers as in nukes. Powers as in the fate of the world is in your hands.'

'Well, OK then, I believe you,' said Obama...wink, wink, 'Bobar.'

Mr. Man magically disappeared back into the land of mans. Obama was freed from the pillowcase, made out of pillowcases. He went back to the Blackhouse and snuggled on the sofa because that is where he lives. The Black House. Indeed.

CHAPTER 2: DOING GOD THINGS

One morning, ten years after the first chapter, Obama thought back to how much of a fool Mr. Man had been that day when he told him he had powers. A big birthday cake that Obama had received for his first birthday (which had been chucked away as he wanted cheese instead) magically reappeared in front of him. Obama thought this must have been a sign for him to eat cheese again. He rushed to the cheese box, but the cake stopped him, as it was now alive and a living organism. Which is the same thing. I think. Obama was confused as cakes aren't usually alive, unless you put Obama's magical ingredient in it which you don't really want to know. The cake said to Obama, 'You have magical powers. You are the one bringing me to life. Eat cheese if you want but don't give anyone emotional damage. You may regret it.' The cake vanished. Obama immediately went out to give emotional damage; he was trying to prove the cake from his first birthday wrong. He decided to give emotional damage to Barney. "Ur Mom doesn't love you. Ur grandma hates you. Ur dad left you. Ur gonna grow up to be Adam Sandler." Obama sang. He remembered this song from a YouTube video he once watched. Barney replied, "How rude! Teleport Obama the Doge to...THE LAND OF THE GODS!!!!"

Obama was being sucked through a giant portal made of cheese. It was taking him to the land of the gods. Obama tried to resist but he couldn't as the portal was made of cheese. He ended up resisting after eating one or two slices of cheese. The mutation that turns him into spirit form to enter the land of the gods had corrupted. Obama wasn't turning into his ghost, spirit form. He was turning into...a god! Obama tried to escape the portal but it was too late. He was in the land of the gods. He was greeted by the cheese god who thought Obama was just an ordinary god who he had never met before. Obama wasn't just an ordinary god; he had mutated into the god of everything – the most powerful god to ever exist. He really wanted to escape from the land of the gods but he didn't know how to use his powers yet so Obama trained for weeks inside the land of the gods (imagine a montage of this awesome training). He finally figured out how to open up the portal to the world of Htrae. Obama opened up the portal and he was sucked in; he was back on Htrae. He had learned some new god things, like: he may not have been the first god of everything but he certainly is a god.

Hang on, I'm just getting a drink.

OK, I'm back.

Obama suddenly, just kidding – it took him a while, walked back from Africa all the way to America. If you're wondering how he got across the ocean, well he's a god, so, he would obviously know how to do that.

When he was back at the Black House he just sat there, continuing his philosophy on thinking. After about 2 hours, he got off his lazy buttocks and started to walk around the city. He saw someone's house that was on fire. He thought super hard about water on that fire and straight away, it started hammering it down, putting the fire out. Obama then did a super goodness charge (a big spin where he spreads everything good throughout the city). Everyone cheered for Obama to be the everything god.

CHAPTER 3: THE GOOD OF THE WORLD

Obama loved what he was doing with his spinning super goodness charge. He thought to himself, *'Why not do some stuff with my general, alien life?'* Obama went back home to the Black House and then he magically created an Xbox Obama-style. On the right panel, there was a picture of a dog. A green one. On the front was a picture of a fly and on the left panel was a picture of a monster from Jupiter. Hence, Obama style. But what was strange about this Xbox, was that it was alive.

"Bobar," said the Xbox.

"Bobar," Obama said back.

The Xbox told him that, "If you really want to have some fun then you must join me into the dark side and manipulate people's minds into playing games or whatever gods do." Obama shouted, "No!" and he tried to destroy the Xbox but the Xbox could move and walked out of the way.

Obama tried to get Barney to help but he was at the supermarket, crying, as Obama had given him emotional damage. Barney didn't know that Obama was a god or even that he was back from the land of the gods yet. He thought that this may be the end for Obama the Doge but he was wrong as Obama had another friend. The cake from his first birthday party. It had magically reappeared in front of the Xbox and mushed itself into the appliance. Obama cheered, "Hooray!" but it was too late. The Xbox had injected Obama with the magical, dark side poison.

Obama started turning black as his mind got manipulated into the forces of evil. A little bit like Darth Vader but much less

THE ADVENTURES OF OBAMA THE GOD

exciting. Obama thought to himself, *'This is the end of Obama the god'.* But, yet again, Obama was wrong. He was not killed. He was just on the dark side. He immediately felt the urge to do bad things. First of all, he took off his dog costume and, as a fly, he was no longer Obama the Doge. He built another costume. He was now...Barack Obama. Well, he wasn't Barack Obama. He just looked like him but that still counts. He magically teleported to the White House. On Earth. Not Htrae and not the Black House.

Obama decided to visit the room which held Joe Biden and replaced him with Obama. Again. He was going to be president again. He did exactly that with his magical, evil, god-like powers. Joe Biden went back to being a zombie wee monster, even though he was never actually a zombie wee monster in the first place; he was part of TSOW (The Survivors of Wee). Obama had started the wee apocalypse all over again but in the real world. He went to the president's ice-cream button and pressed it to get infinite ice-cream. A cheese flavoured ice-cream because both Obama's love cheese, right? Right? Right??? Anyways, Obama randomly decided to launch a nuke onto Htrae; this way Obama could do bad things to his planet without anyone knowing.

All of a sudden, the door to the White house EXPLODED!!! Obama knew it must be the zombie wee monsters - they had broken in. But let's not forget that Obama is a god (The book is called Obama the God). Obama took on the wee monsters but he failed to take away the wee venom and was bitten! So he was a Super Evil Zombie Wee monster. Luckily for the good people that are out there...BARNEY HAD ARRIVED!!! While he was at the shop, he had learnt kung fu moves and was fighting for his and Obama's lives! Barney won the fight and only had to cure Obama now. Not really though, all the zombie wee monsters got cured and Obama was no longer evil - just like in the last book.

So the good of the world saved Obama!!!

CHAPTER 4: THE GAMING PHASE

Obama was very upset about almost killing Barney when he started the apocalypse. So much so, that he went home to the Black House and didn't return for between 10 and 20 months. But don't worry, on Htrae, people don't age. Except for Barney because he comes from a different world. Whilst Obama was in the Black House, he realiused that the Xbox, that the cake had squished itself into, was still working, so he decided to give it a try with his new god powers. Whilst picking it up, he said, "Bobar, old friend. Nice to see you again." Obama set up the Xbox and was signing into his account when the Xbox flickered, and teleported, and turned into a Playstation. He didn't really care. He just wanted to see what games he could download and what would happen now he had been charmed with the god-effect. He signed into his Playstation account which, since he was a god, he could just magically create. Obama downloaded Fortnite.

DING DONG! Paula Parcels was at the door. He rushed as quicky as he could because Paula Parcels was evil if he was late to the door. She would smack him in the face with his own parcel if he was late. It had happened before. Sadly, Obama did not make it to the door in time and, not surprisingly, Paula Parcels whacked him in the face with his own parcel. Obama wasn't sure what the parcel was as he hadn't ordered anything. He had the horrible job of checking to see if the parcel had broken. Luckily, it hadn't as it had an indestructable sign on it. He automatically knew it was an accessory for the Xbox, I mean Playstation, but the second he plugged it in, his godspidey-sense kicked in and he was told that this was a scam. But, he was wrong. He was wrong to think that this was just a normal USB extension. Obviously, Obama just ignored it with the crazy mind he has.

Obama began to play Fortnite but it wasn't the most usual game of Fortnite. Everyone was way better than him, which was impossible, as he had been grinding. Then, Obama was knocked out in place 99 when he had killed 9 people. Obama thought something was wrong but didn't do anything about it. He gamed and gamed until his fingers stopped working!

Then, an evil man, named Dan, came in the front door of the Black House (they really should get their security sorted out) and tried to touch Obama and turn him into a cheesecake. The recipe for this cheesecake is as follows:

Ingredients

- 250g digestive biscuits

- 100g butter, melted
- 1 vanilla pod
- 600g full fat soft cheese
- 100g icing sugar
- 284ml pot of double cream

For the topping
- 400g punnet of strawberries, halved
- 25g icing sugar

Method

STEP 1

To make the base, butter and line a 23cm loose-bottomed tin with baking parchment. Put the digestive biscuits in a plastic food bag and crush to crumbs using a rolling pin. Transfer the crumbs to a bowl, then pour over the melted butter. Mix thoroughly until the crumbs are completely coated. Tip them into the prepared tin and press firmly down into the base to create an even layer.

Chill in the fridge for 1 hr to set firmly.

STEP 2

Slice the vanilla pod in half lengthways, leaving the tip intact, so that the two halves are still joined. Holding onto the tip of the pod, scrape out the seeds using the back of a kitchen knife.

STEP 3

Pour the double cream into a bowl and whisk with an electric mixer until it's just starting to thicken to soft peaks. Place the soft cheese, icing sugar and the vanilla seeds in a separate bowl, then beat for 2 mins with an electric mixer until smooth and starting to thicken, it will get thin and then start to thicken again. Tip in the double cream and fold it into the soft cheese mix. You're looking for it to be thickened enough to hold its shape when you tip a spoon of it upside down. If it's not thick enough, continue to whisk. Spoon onto the biscuit base, starting from the edges and working inwards, making sure that there are no air bubbles. Smooth the top of the cheesecake down with the back of a dessert spoon or spatula. Leave to set in the fridge overnight.

STEP 4

Bring the cheesecake to room temperature about 30 mins before serving. To remove it from the tin, place the base on top of a can, then gradually pull the sides of the tin down. Slip the cake onto a serving plate, removing the lining paper and base. Purée half the strawberries in a blender or food processor with the icing sugar and 1 tsp water, then sieve. Pile the remaining strawberries onto the cake, and pour the purée over the top.

BBC GoodFood. August 2007. *Strawberry cheesecake in 4 easy steps.*

Accessed 24th July 2024.

https://www.bbcgoodfood.com/recipes/strawberry-cheesecake-4-easy-steps

Well, I bet you didn't expect to get a

cheesecake recipe in this book...except you did, as I told you I would put it in, at the start.

Anyway, back to the story. Dan leapt out to try to touch Obama but the second he did, Barney jumped in the way. Barney was now a cheesecake. Don't worry, Obama made Dan disappear out of the book forever, and he will not appear in any book I may, or may not, write in the future. Obama then freed Barney from the curse and turned him back into a dog.

CHAPTER 5: THE RETURN OF THE ORIGINAL OBAMA

Eventually, after the cheesecake incident, Obama realised that he was in the North Pacific Ocean so he used his god-like powers to magically disappear from the ocean and into the Black House. When he was there, he realised the USB stick that went into the Xbox/Playstation, that evil, evil Paula Parcels gave him, and Dan coming to try to turn him into a cheesecake, all matched up. Dan and Paula Parcels were friends and what that USB did, was tell Dan where Obama was. Obama suddenly danced around and Mr. Man and Mrs. Woman were there and they exploded into marshmallows. You may remember from the the first book that this meant someone was controlling them and something had malfunctioned. But, unlike the last book, we are actually going to find out...

Hang on. BRB. Just going to the toilet.

Hi, I'm back. So the mastermind behind all the mischief... **Barney!?**

Yes, Barney had set up mind controllers into Mr. Man and Mrs. Woman to track Obama!!! After all of this happened, Obama thought to himself to introduce Barney to his other doge friends (Buzz & Baxter). And so he did. They all liked each other, except for the doges and the cats (Spooky & Nessie). They didn't like each other at all. Because the doges chase the cats! Buzz was okay at not chasing. Then there were Barney and Baxter. Obama was pretty chill though. They all hung out for a bit (not Nessie

& Spooky) untill it was time to go home. "Bobar," said Obama to his friends and walked home with Barney. After they got home, Obama thought to himself, 'I wonder if I could make wishes come true?' He tried it. "I WISH I WAS A REAL GREEN DOG!!!" All of a sudden, Obama couldn't take of his head and wasn't a god anymore.

THE END!!!